HERGÉ

The Tintin Games Book

Methuen Children's Books

It's no use running...

Object of the game: Tintin must catch Snowy.

How to play: One player is Tintin, the other is Snowy. Tintin places his counter on the first picture and plays first. At each go he moves two squares, horizontally, vertically, or one square in each direction. Snowy must run away from Tintin. He places his counter on the last picture and moves one square at each go, but in all directions, including diagonally. Take care! Tintin and Snowy are forbidden to enter the red squares. The game ends when Tintin catches Snowy.

Find the mistakes

There are 30 mistakes in this drawing; see if you can find them all! (Solution on page 30.)

Coo-ee, where are you?

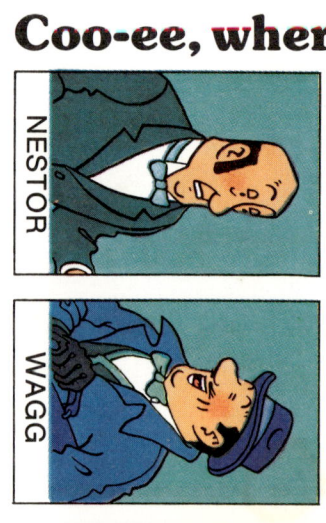

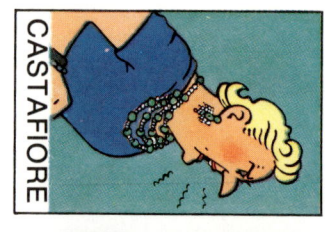

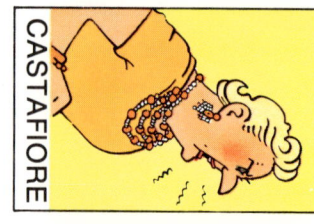

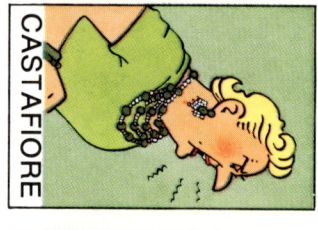
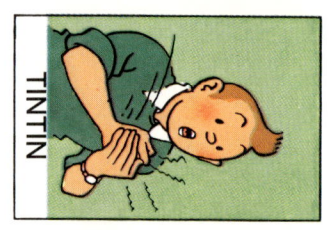

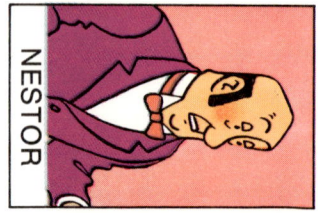

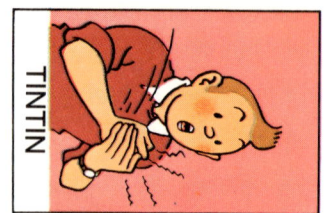

Arrange the book so that one player is looking at page 8 and the other is looking at page 11. Hold page 9 vertically to hide your game.

Calculus' wardrobe

Coo-ee, where are you?

Object of the game: To collect six counters on your page.

How to play: Place your four counters in four squares, grouped in twos. Each pair of counters must be horizontal or vertical, not diagonal. The two pairs must not touch, even at the corners. The first player chooses a square in his opponent's game, naming the character and the colour of the square e.g. Calculus, blue. If the square is empty, then the second player has his turn. If the square is occupied by a counter, the first player claims it. He keeps it in reserve until he has taken a second counter from his opponent; then he can put this new pair on his page.

Each person's turn lasts for as long as he scores with his choice of square. The player who collects six counters (three pairs) on his page is the winner. It is a good idea to make a plan of the game in order to record the moves scored against your opponent.

Calculus' wardrobe

Find the two pictures on pages 9 and 10 where Calculus is wearing the same clothes. (Solution on page 30.)

9

Calculus' wardrobe

Calculus' wardrobe

Find the two pictures on pages 9 and 10 where Calculus is wearing the same clothes. (Solution on page 30.)

Coo-ee, where are you?

Object of the game: To collect six counters on your page.

How to play: Place your four counters in four squares, grouped in twos. Each pair of counters must be horizontal or vertical, not diagonal. The two pairs must not touch, even at the corners. The first player chooses a square in his opponent's game, naming the character and the colour of the square e.g. Calculus, blue. If the square chosen is empty, then the second player has his turn. If the square is occupied by a counter, the first player claims it. He keeps it in reserve until he has taken a second counter from his opponent; then he can put this new pair on his page.

Each person's turn lasts for as long as he scores with his choice of square. The player who collects six counters (three pairs) on his page is the winner. It is a good idea to make a plan of the game in order to record the moves scored against your opponent.

Coo-ee, where are you?

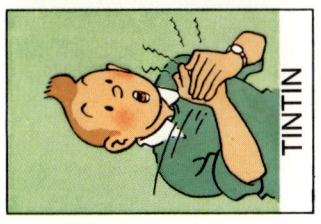 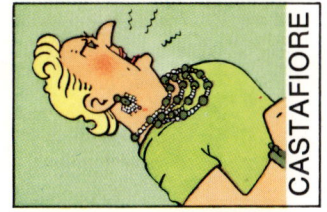  

 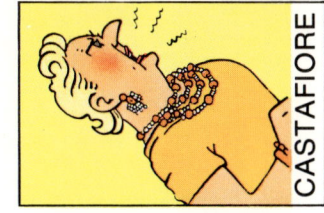  

Arrange the book so that one player is looking at page 8 and the other is looking at page 11.
Hold page 9 vertically to hide your game.

Conversations

A. I . . . I . . . w-was g-g-going t-t-to t-tell y-y-you, b-b-but y-y-you in-in-inter-inter-interrupted m-m-me! . . . He st-st-stopped at . . . at . . . at . . . th-th-the Co-Co-Co . . .
B. Where's the young foreigner you are taking to Klow?
C. L-l-l-listen . . . I . . . I . . . I'm . . . I'm . . .
D. Look out! . . . Here they come! . . .
E. Quiet! . . . I can hear a car.
F. Hello? . . . Yes, this is Wiskitotz . . . Ah! It's you Sirov . . . Well? What? . . . Szplug! . . . So it's not your fault? . . . Perhaps you think it's mine, eh? What? . . . If he hadn't stuttered so? If! . . . If! . . . You can get round anything with "if" . . . I'll telephone to the Chief of police at Zlip . . . Yes, he's one of us . . . He'll stop him on the road.
G. I . . . I'm t-t-trying to t-t-tell yy-yy-yyou . . . th-th-the y-y-young f-f-for-foreigner w-w
H. Hands up!
I. Was w-w-w-with m-m-me?
J. It's gone . . . We can go back.
K. W-w-was in . . . in . . . in th-th-that c-c-car w-w-w-which j-j-just papa-papa-passed!
L. Hello? Yes, this is Sirov . . . Hello Wiskitotz . . . Yes . . . a young boy, on the road to Klow . . . In a peasant's cart . . . Good, we'll be waiting in the forest . . . Yes, we'll leave at once . . . Goodbye!
M. Th-th-the young f-f-f-foreigner . . .
N. The Co-Co-Coach-Coachman's Rest, an-an-and . . .
O. If you say one word, or make one move . . . just remember our rifles are trained on you!
P. Szplug! Where can he be? . . . Come on, are you going to talk?
Q. N-n-no! . . . It . . . It . . . it-it-s b-b-be-because
I . . . I . . . I . . . t-t-talk . . . talk . . . talk . . .
R. That's enough! . . . We know he's with you! . . . Search the cart, Zlop!
S. An-an-and he-he . . . he . . . g-g-g-
T. What makes you stutter like that? . . . Fear?
U. Splitz on Szplug! Where is he? . . .
V. Cocoa! . . . Cocoa! . . . What cocoa? . . . Have you been drinking?
W. Sirov! There's no one there!
X. Th-th-the f-f-foreigner who . . . who w-w-w- . . .
Y. Hello? . . . Yes, this is Klow 3324 . . . Yes, Central Committee . . . Trovik speaking . . . Oh it's you, Wiskitotz . . . What? . . . Tintin? . . . But that's impossible: the pilot has just told me . . . What? . . . Into some straw! . . . Szplug! He must be prevented from reaching Klow at all costs! . . . Do it how you like . . . Yes, ring up Sirov.
Z. Why didn't you say so sooner?

Put each piece of dialogue into its correct box. (Solution on page 30.)

Missing objects

Object of the game: To match separate objects with the correct pictures.

How to play: Each player chooses one of the squares, A B C D, on page 15. He must find the pictures which contain his objects and write down his answers e.g. A 13 – picture 17. The first player to complete his list has a bonus of 6 points, the second player gets 4 points and the third 2 points. Take care! Once a player has declared 'Finished', he cannot alter his answers. When all the players have finished, check the answers on page 30. For each correct answer, each player adds one point to his bonus. The player with the most points wins the game.

"Look, there's the case... sniff... exactly where I put it."

Calculus is kidnapped

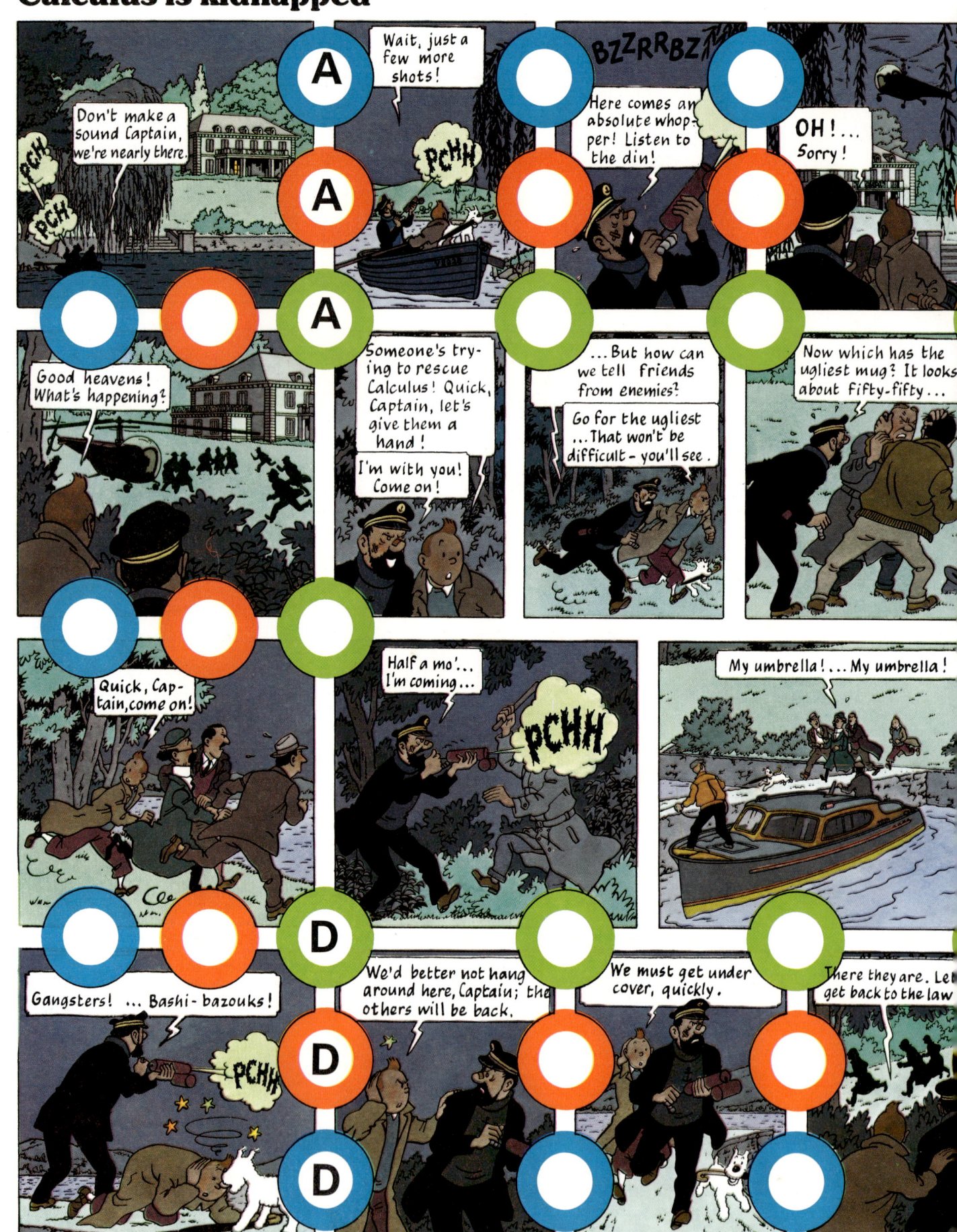

Object of the game: Complete the three circuits (green, red and blue) to escape the kidnappers.

How to play: Each player chooses one of the four letters, A B C D, and places his three counters on the circles marked with the chosen letter. Begin with the green circuit. Play is in alphabetical order and the counters move clockwise. Player A throws the dice and moves his counter first, only on the green circles. The other players in turn do likewise. Each player must complete his green circuit by returning to his starting point. Take care! In order to finish, the exact number must be thrown to reach the starting

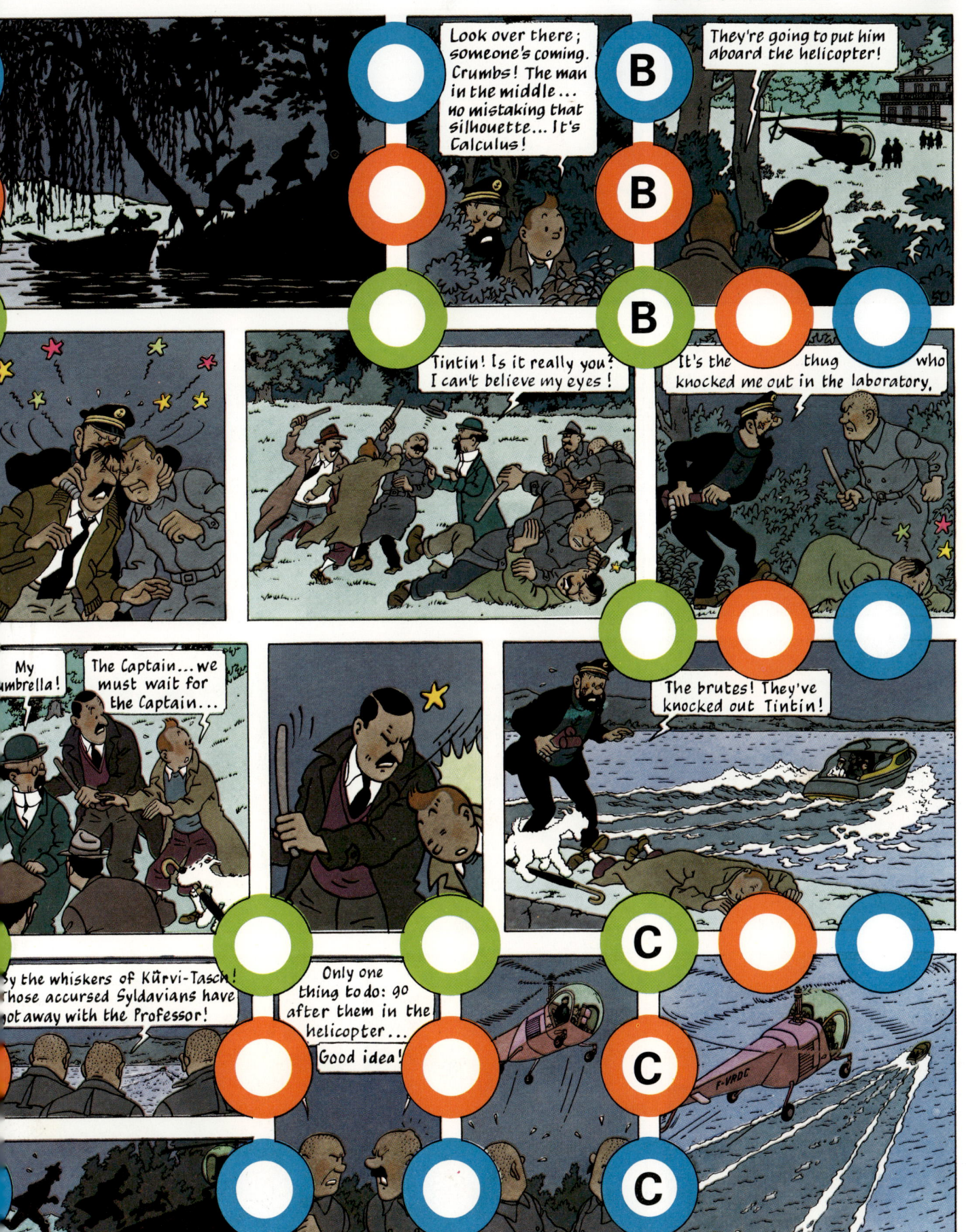

point, otherwise the counter moves backwards for as many circles as there are surplus points on the dice. When a player has completed his green circuit, he withdraws that counter from the game and plays first the red circuit, then the blue circuit. If a player lands on a circle which is already occupied, then the last to arrive is sent back to his starting point. If this player has already completed one or two circuits, he must return the counters to their starting points and begin the game again. The winner is the first person to complete the three circuits.

The battle of Zileheroum

Object of the game: To reassemble your troops in a straight line, either horizontal, vertical or diagonal.

How to play: The first player places two counters in the two upper corners. The other player places two counters in the two lower corners. Each player then places his third counter in the empty square between his opponent's two counters, so that each player's three counters are arranged in a triangle. Each player in turn moves a counter one square at a time in any direction, horizontal, vertical or diagonal, in order to reassemble his counters, or troops, in a line. Take care! You cannot move across an occupied square or land upon it.

Souvenirs of Sbrodj

Souvenirs of Sbrodj

Object of the game: To identify the object chosen as a souvenir.

How to play: One player chooses the souvenir. He holds this page vertically between him and the other players, who will be the questioners. The first player then secretly chooses a face, a hand or a foot of a character in one of the pictures and writes it down on a piece of paper. Each questioner asks only one question at a time, in an attempt to find the chosen part. But he must not mention either the numbers of the pictures, the names of the characters, or the words 'face, hand or foot'. The player who is being questioned must only answer yes or no. Each questioner is allowed one identification of the souvenir e.g. 'It is Captain Haddock's head in picture 1.' If he is wrong, he is disqualified. If his answer is correct, he wins a point and it is his turn to choose the souvenir. The winner is the player with the most points.

Souvenirs of Sbrodj

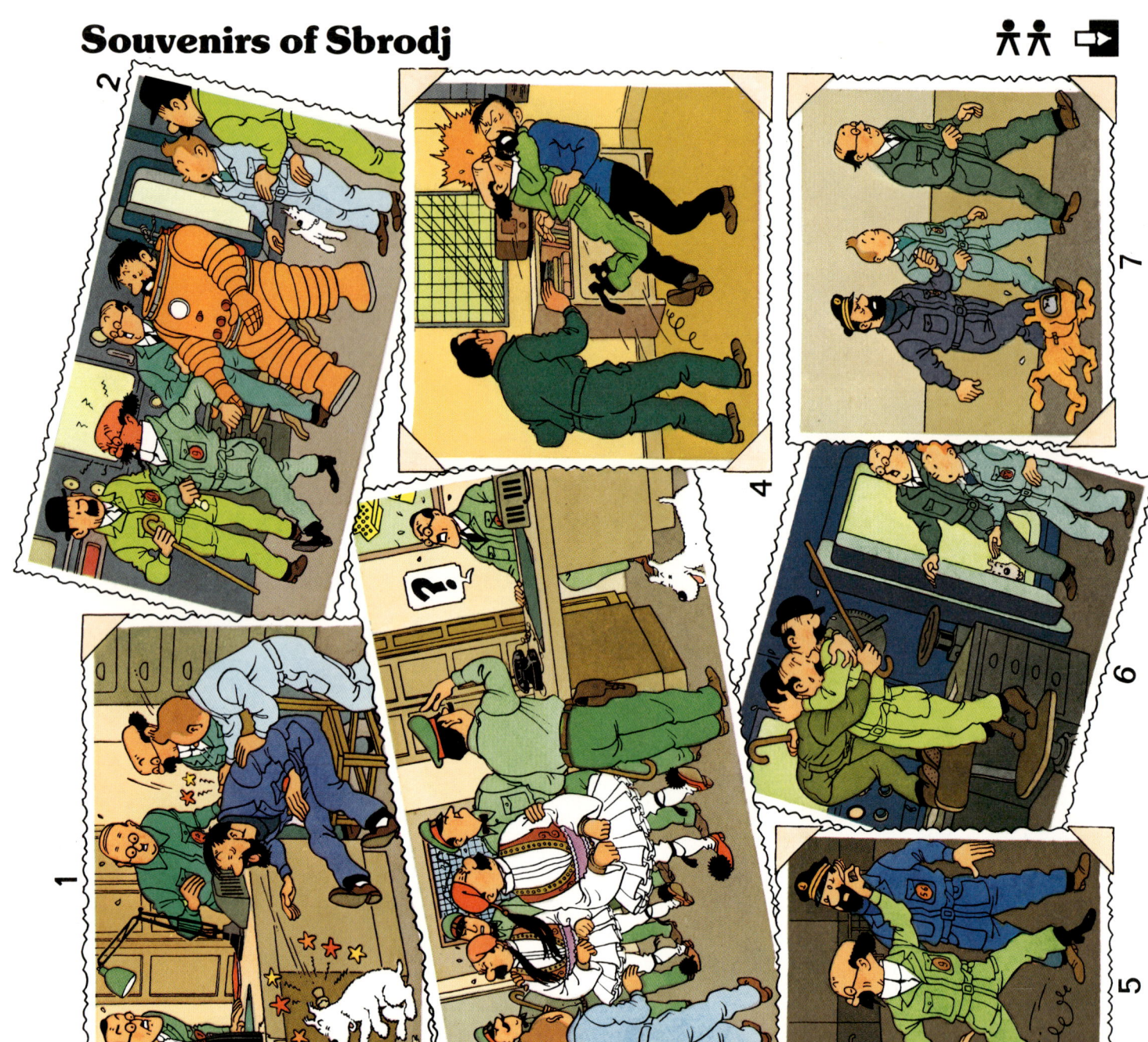

Object of the game: To identify the object chosen as a souvenir.

How to play: One player chooses the souvenir. He holds this page vertically between him and the other players, who will be the questioners. The first player then secretly chooses a face, a hand or a foot of a character in one of the pictures and writes it down on a piece of paper. Each questioner asks only one question at a time, in an attempt to find the chosen part. But he must not mention either the numbers of the pictures, the names of the characters, or the words 'face, hand or foot'. The player who is being questioned must only answer yes or no. Each questioner is allowed one identification of the souvenir e.g. 'It is Captain Haddock's head in picture 1.' If he is wrong, he is disqualified. If his answer is correct, he wins a point and it is his turn to choose the souvenir. The winner is the player with the most points.

Secret pictures

Object of the game: To track down your opponents' secret pictures.

How to play: Each player secretly chooses a picture and writes its number on a 'secret paper'. Each player in turn asks one of his opponents a question e.g. 'Is Tintin running in your picture?' Take care! You must answer truthfully. The same player cannot be questioned twice running. When a player thinks he knows the secret pictures of all his opponents, he writes their numbers at the bottom of his secret paper and checks them against the other secret papers. If all the numbers are correct, he has won and the game is over. If not, he will no longer be able to ask questions, but he must answer his opponents until the end of the game.

The Marlinspike letters

A B C D E F G H I J K L M N O P Q R S T U V

Object of the game: To reach the last letter without hesitating.

How to play: Each player chooses a picture. Then each player in turn describes, in a single word, a situation or an object shown in his picture. This word must begin with A the first time, B the second and so on.

Examples: *top picture*: Armchair, Ankle, Ace; *bottom picture*: Avenue, Awning, Awaiting
If a player cannot think of a word, he misses his turn. He must catch up on the next turn by giving two words beginning with the next letter. If he cannot do this, he is disqualified.

The Captain's excursion

Object of the game: To overcome the obstacles and be the first to reach square 27.

How to play: Start at square 1. Each player throws the dice in turn and moves his counter forward the correct number of squares. The players must obey the instructions of the squares they land on. When a player lands on an occupied square, the newcomer sends the other back to the start. In order to win, a player must throw the exact number needed to reach square 27. Otherwise, the player moves backwards for as many squares as there are surplus points on the dice.

Saint Vladimir's Day

Object of the game: To reassemble the royal procession which is riding through the Syldavian capital on Saint Vladimir's Day.

How to play: Each player draws a grid of 24 squares (6 x 4) on his paper and reassembles the scene, writing each number in its correct place. When the players have finished, they check their answers against the solution on page 30. The winner is the player who reconstructs the scene correctly in the shortest time.

The chase in the crypt

Put the pictures in their correct story sequence. (Solution on page 30.)

Solution to the games

Find the mistakes (pages 6 and 7):
1 Tap on the ladder of the television broadcasting van.
2 A fir tree branch on the oak tree.
3 The clock on the van.
4 "FISH & CHIPS" on the ice-cream seller's van.
5 The passenger in the car is facing backwards.
6 The three-armed customer.
7 PHOTOS written upside down.
8 "MARSLINPIKE" is spelt wrongly.
9 The lady is not holding her handbag.
10 The pram has three wheels.
11 The key in the vendor's back.
12 The soles of the picnicker's shoes.
13 The cut braces.
14 The knapsack suspended in mid-air.
15 The cooker on the man's back.
16 The one-legged boy scout.
17 The vendor walking on three legs.
18 The one-armed camera technician.
19 The red car with no back wheel.
20 The steering wheel in the back of the red car.
21 The figures on the number plate are back to front.
22 The policeman in shorts.
23 The balloons without strings.
24 The stone balls on the gateway.
25 The missing rung on the cine photographer's ladder.
26 The scooter's handlebars.
27 "RAMBURGERS" should be HAMBURGERS.
28 The telescope is the wrong way round.
29 The hamburger van's chimney is separated from its cowl.
30 The tent pole is incomplete.

Calculus' wardrobe (pages 9 and 10): 9 and 16.

Conversations (pages 12 and 13):

1 – Y	6 – M	11 – Q	16 – N	21 – C
2 – L	7 – R	12 – W	17 – Z	22 – J
3 – D	8 – X	13 – P	18 – E	23 – G
4 – H	9 – I	14 – A	19 – S	24 – U
5 – B	10 – T	15 – V	20 – O	25 – K

Missing objects (pages 14 and 15):

A 1 – 10	B 1 – 14	C 1 – 6	D 1 – 6
A 2 – 14	B 2 – 16	C 2 – 11	D 2 – 10
A 3 – 12	B 3 – 6	C 3 – 16	D 3 – 5
A 4 – 13	B 4 – 2	C 4 – 13	D 4 – 14
A 5 – 10	B 5 – 8	C 5 – 8	D 5 – 8
A 6 – 14	B 6 – 3	C 6 – 3	D 6 – 9
A 7 – 12	B 7 – 5	C 7 – 13	D 7 – 7
A 8 – 6	B 8 – 13	C 8 – 6	D 8 – 2
A 9 – 13	B 9 – 11	C 9 – 14	D 9 – 4
A 10 – 8	B 10 – 6	C 10 – 5	D 10 – 9
A 11 – 15	B 11 – 1	C 11 – 13	D 11 – 7
A 12 – 10	B 12 – 1	C 12 – 4	D 12 – 15

Saint Vladimir's Day (pages 26 and 27):

11	13	10	3	22	14
16	24	20	5	12	1
8	23	6	18	4	15
21	9	7	19	17	2

The chase in the crypt (pages 28 and 29):
8 – 11 – 6 – 22 – 3 – 21 – 23 – 17 – 10 – 5 – 19 – 12 – 2 – 18 – 15 – 14 – 13 – 9 – 16 – 1 – 7 – 20 – 4